My Hanukkah

Monica Hughes

Raintree

Chicago, Illinois

Printed and bound in the United States at Lake Book Manufacturing, Inc.
07 06 05 04 03
10 9 8 7 6 5 4 3 2 1

Library of Congress Cataloging-in-Publication Data:
Hughes, Monica.
  My Hanukkah / Monica Hughes.
      p. cm. -- (Festivals)
Summary: Illustrations and simple text describe how one family
celebrates Hanukkah.
  ISBN 1-4109-0638-8 (hc) -- ISBN 1-4109-0664-7 (pbk.)
  1. Hanukkah--Juvenile literature. [1. Hanukkah. 2. Holidays.] I.
Title. II. Series: Hughes, Monica. Festivals.
  BM695.H3H84 2004
  296.4'35--dc21
                                        2003010853

Acknowledgments
The Publishers would like to thank p. 12 Getty Images\Larry Eatz and p. 19 Chris Schwarz and Getty Images\Alex Wong
for permission to reproduce photographs.

Cover photograph of the family meal, reproduced with permission of Chris Schwarz.

Every effort has been made to contact copyright holders of any material reproduced in this book.
Any omissions will be rectified in subsequent printings if notice is given to the publishers.

Some words are shown in bold, **like this.** You can find out
what they mean by looking in the glossary on page 24.

Contents

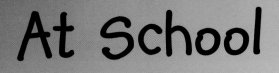

Hanukkah is almost here!
We make decorations at school.

4

Our teacher reads the Hanukkah story.

Hanukkah Treats

At home we make applesauce for **Hanukkah.**

We make jelly doughnuts, too.

7

Cooking Latkes

We help Mom make **latkes**.

Latkes are potato pancakes.

9

Hanukkah Lights

Every night, we light candles in the **hanukiah**.

This big hanukiah
has electric lights.

11

Eight Nights

Hanukkah lasts for eight nights.
We need one candle for each night.

shamash

Every night, we add a new candle in the **hanukiah.**

Mom lights them with the **shamash.**

Hanukkah Clothes

We wear our very best clothes for **Hanukkah.**

Hanukkah Presents

We get a present each night of Hanukkah.

How many presents do we get?

Celebrating Hanukkah

First, we light the candles
and say a prayer.

Then, we eat our **Hanukkah** meal.

Do you remember what we are eating?

19

The Dreidel Game

dreidel

We play the **dreidel** game.

First, we spin the dreidel.

We win chocolate money called **gelt**.
My grandpa helps us play.

A Hanukkah Party

We are going to a **Hanukkah** party.

We sing songs and play games.

23

Glossary

dreidel (You say DRAY-dl.) a spinning top with four sides. Each side shows a different letter from the Hebrew alphabet.

gelt chocolate candy wrapped up to look like gold coins

hanukiah (You say hah-NOO-kee-uh.) a candle holder that has places for nine candles. Some people call the hanukiah a menorah.

Hanukkah (You say HAH-nah-kuh.) the Jewish festival of lights, celebrated in November or December

kippot (You say KIP-puht; one is a KIP-uh.) small, round cap that Jewish boys and men wear to cover their heads, also called a yarmulke

latkes pancakes made with potatoes and flour that are fried in oil

shamash the extra (ninth) candle in the hanukiah. It is also called the servant candle and is used to light the other candles.

Index